Prejudice
And Pride

I0117226

Katie Haigh

chipmunkapublishing

the mental health publisher

Published by

Chipmunkapublishing

PO Box 6872

Brentwood

Essex CM13 1ZT

United Kingdom

http://www.chipmunkapublishing.com

Copyright © Katie Haigh 2012

Edited by Thet San Soe

ISBN   978-1-84991-863-3

Chipmunkapublishing gratefully acknowledge the support of Arts Council England.

A Day on the Street of a Mobility Scooter

It was supposed to make life easier.
To give me more freedom,
Less pain.
When it arrived,
I had such hope,
Knowing I would no longer feel trapped.

The day had started quite simply.
Reversing out of the garage,
I reached the road.
My heart dropped.
The crossing further up wasn't lowered.
So I had to cross at a dangerous point,
Timing it with fast-moving traffic.

When I finally crossed,
My bubble soon burst
When I reached the Morrison's crossing.
Getting to the middle was easy,
But the curb on the last bit wasn't low.
So I had to travel up the road,
Fearing my scooter and traffic would collide.

Once on the path,
My relief was short-lived.
Heading towards me were a couple and child,
Hand in hand, taking up every inch of the path.
I tried with frustration to pass by them,
But was greeted with irritated scowls.
They wanted me to fly over!
Now that's impossible to do.

Finally I reached the revolving doors
And waited until my path was clear.
Yet as I set off,
A lady jumped in my path,
And someone with a trolley was behind.
Manoeuvring in such a small space
Wasn't easy to do.

I ended up bashing her heels.
I hadn't meant to.
Yet annoyance niggled.
If only they'd left my path clear.
Inside the supermarket,
You'd expect it be easy.
The problems weren't over yet.

First up was dodging disgruntled shoppers,
Trolleys overflowing from their shopping.
Second, the bakery-counter so high,
I had to shout what I wanted
And catch my bag of pies and sausage rolls.
Thirdly the little tots,
Whom I tried not to bash as they ran.
They toddled unsupervised
While parents chatting oblivious.
The aisles were actually wide enough,
Until baskets brimming with merchandise were added.
To make us want to buy, buy, buy.
But I couldn't get past, past, past.
So I had to reverse
Into angry mutterings;
People wishing I simply wasn't there.

Checking out was relatively easy,
With helpful staff seeing to my needs.

But then it's time for the journey home,
Either against traffic or a long way 'round.
Heading back down Bamford Road,
Crossing at the same risky point,
Parking up in the garage,
Feeling frazzled, stressed out.
Not in the least pain-free.
It was supposed to make life easier.
It is a shame the outside world disagrees.

Disabled Choice

You stop. You stare.
You laugh. You judge.
A young woman on a scooter;
It doesn't add up.
She's too young to be disabled,
To be in pain in any way,
To struggle physically,
To feel low and strained.
Stiff joints and walking sticks
Are for the old.
How dare she fake it!
She's a benefit fraud!
On the outside
There're no scars.
No missing limbs.
She's a liar,
A deceiver,
And a weaver of webs.
But what you don't see
Are her daily struggle
With simple tasks;
Her wide awaking with discomfort
In the middle of the night;
Her tears of frustration
For things she cannot do;
The tablets she takes
To help her see the day through.
So next time you see her,
Think of what you choose not to see.
A woman who's disabled
Is not the way
She decided to be.

Limitless

The limitations of pain,
Draining energy,
Sucking the joy out of a moment;
You can fight it.
Think positive.
Build a wall.
Yet pain will chisel and chip away,
Creating stone from brick,
Heavy weight upon shoulders,
As constant,
Sharp, shooting, pulsations
Wrack my body.
Muscles tremble.
My spine shakes.
I ache,
And I pray
To some greater being.
Who can release me?
Free me
From the limitations of pain.

The Layers of Immobility

If you want to feel immobility,
Imagine being restrained,
Cramped and contained within a wooden box,
Twisted into awkward shapes,
Dark and alone.
Salvation just out of reach,
Teasing your fingertips.

If you want to embrace immobility,
Step into a freezing lake.
Feel its icy touch.
Absorb it deep into your spine.
As it leaves you unable to move,
Skin cold like marble.

If you want to have immobility,
Look beyond disabled eyes.
Observe what you cannot see.
Notice the invisible.
See what others won't.

Because immobility
Is like vapour.
We breathe it in
Without inhaling its substance,
Not understanding
The core of immobility.

Pain

Sometimes I just want it to stop.
My minds screaming, "I've had enough!"
The pain just won't go away.
Every second. Every moment.
Every day.
Like a virus,
It's under my skin,
Gradually tearing me apart from within.
Yet outwards, I look fine.
People can't see what's happening inside.
They see me through veiled eyes,
Missing the problems I hide.
Popping pills to take it away,
Gels and creams for every ache.
I try to keep myself strong.
Think positive.
Can't do wrong.
Yet still the pain chips away,
Making a challenge every day.
I accept there'll never be a cure.
There'll be good days,
And bad days for sure.
So I just keep living for today
Because I know my pain
Is here to stay.

Pills Melt in Vinegar

They come in white, yellow
And blue.
In powders.
In syringes.
Doses so high they kill.
In boxes.
In shops.
Or in darkened street corners.
They numb.
They energise.
They fulfil deep desires.
They enable.
Disable.
Bring highs and lows.
They make vulnerable, paranoid.
Can help reach personal goals.
They buzz.
Make well.
Make ill,
Desperate and worried.
They hurt.
They kill.
They destroy families.
Ask yourself really,
"Do I need that next hit?"
Because pills melt in vinegar,
So dissolve all the shit!

The Battle Within

The light within you dims,
Reflected on glazed eyes.
Emotions bubble and surface,
Yet fight to hide.
You see yourself through others.
Vales of fabricated negativity.
Disorientated self-image.
Harsh self-analysis.
Your individuality increases your likeability.
Your quirks give interesting twists of character.
You are easy to love,
But you have a destructive sense of doubt.
Your mind ticking, ticking.
Creating a world
Within a world.
Within a moment of time
You are trapped
By invisible walls,
Isolating the happiness
You yearn to touch.
To feel.
To have.
To reach out.
Keep stretching out to your dreams,
And one day,
You will be happy,
Being you.

Dedicated to Gemma who is fighting the battle within.

Memoirs of a Housewife

Remember to remember
What is it I have to do?
Make the house sparkle,
Dust, spray and vacuum.
Wash the house from floor to roof.

Remember to remember
Pay all the bills.
Final reminders are unpleasant surprises.

Remember to remember
To iron all the kids' clothes;
Otherwise my mother-in-law is sure to turn her nose up.

Remember to remember
Just what to make for tea;
Remembering always that the kids won't eat peas.

Remember to remember
To make my husband dinner for work.
Because he's a diabetic
Who may pass out.

Remember to remember
To get that birthday present.
Otherwise they'll be in tears
When I arrive empty-handed.

Remember to remember
What it is you have to do.
While keeping yourself together,
Remember to be 'you'.

Invisible

I am the impostor.
The one you cannot see.
I blend into the background.
I exist, but can't be seen.
I watch the world pass by.
See others live their lives,
While I remain transparent.
The quietest voice.
To some I have a title,
Mum, daughter and friend.
Yet within myself I hide.
Afraid to share who I am.
So I continue,
Observing people go by,
Because I am the impostor
In the background of your lives.

Control Food

I don't know when it started.
When food became an issue,
I remember how life was.
I was diagnosed as dyslexic
After Mum sent me for a private test.
Although the school didn't want to accept it,
They didn't want to help.
Budget issues, staffing and resources.
Excuses, excuses and excuses.
My Mum fought their indifference,
Craving the help and guidance I needed.
I heard judgemental whispers,
Rancid gossip from those who demand respect.
During this time,
My brother suffered depression,
So life was stressed.

At school I became wallpaper.
The bullies wouldn't pick on me.
The popular left me alone.
I was a muddle of mishmash words,
So I spoke in low whispers.
They could not make fun of
What they did not hear.
Invisible.
I existed,
Floating through life.
Lost.
Forever falling
Deeper into despair.

The beginning came
With a loss of appetite.
Food offered me no comfort.
I cut my skin.
I wrote down my feelings.
I even tried magic,
Latching onto a childlike essence,
Casting spells of protection,
Wishing for release.
It didn't come.

Homework and coursework weighted me down.
Working until midnight,
Just to keep up with my peers.
I wanted to get good GCSE's.
It irritated me.
My classmates shirked off their work,
Yet they achieved more than me.

Why?
I couldn't understand it.
Eventually exhaustion overtook me.
It was easy to skip meals,
When my mind was overloaded.

It was never about being thin.
I was already thin.
In fact my body lacked curves,
Which lowered my self-esteem more.
I was skinny and pale,
Likened to a corpse.
It hurt.

Yet it only made me eat less.
I needed to control something.
Something I could do.
Something I could be good at.

I became an expert at food avoidance.
I told friends I'd have my dinner at Grandma's,
I told Grandma I'd have dinner at school with friends.
And when I did have to eat with people,
I'd rearrange my meal,
Making it less.
It was a skill.
My biggest achievement
Was the satisfaction of no food for two weeks.
I just wasn't hungry anymore.

The demon was eventually slain.
A breakthrough came
In the form of a new life.
She became my reason
To eat.
To give her substance.
To be her mum.
Yet that devil still stalks me,
With its temptation to control
My life
Food.

Victim of Child Hate

In orchestrating a campaign of hate,
A man with learning difficulties,
Harassed once a week.
Twelve months of antisocial behaviour.
Criminal damage.
Children as young as eight
Terrorising a forty-seven year old man.
Bricks thrown through his windows.
Eggs pelted at his door.
It's hard on him
To communicate.
Children played on that.
Phone calls to the police.
Incident reports.
Targeting a person
Who is different.
It's disgusting!
Police speaking with parents.
The children admitted
It was them.
Reduced to tears
When told their behaviour
Could lead to suicide.
Then came
New incidents.
Could it be
The same children?
Neighbours witnessed harassment,
But also became victims.
Parents don't know
Where their kids played,
What they were doing.
Kids are mischievous.
This is terrible.
Police warning youths.
Hate crime.
Would not be tolerated.
Making an appeal.
Identify these children.
Anyone?
Can contact
Neighbourhood Police.

Self-Destruct

Sometimes I crave it.
That crimson river.
I am pushed and pulled,
Twisted inside.
Just one cut.
It won't hurt.
It will ease the frustration,
Anger and pain.
It will release me.
The sharp cold metal,
Pressed
Until it slices.
Let the blood flow.
I am on the edge,
Ready to let go.
To jump
Into the abyss.
I am no more.
Gone.

Turn me on

Sometimes I find it hard
To turn off
The switch which controls my mind.
When it is off,
And refuses to turn on,
Draining the energy of my brain.
Thoughts become a sluggish sludge.
Barely visible imagery,
Clearly blurred.
Yet when the switch is on,
My mind will
Tick, tick, tick,
With thoughts
And talk in a thousand words.
Things to do.
Remember
Lists and bills.
Children to entertain,
Feed, wash and bathe.
Then I hit the wall.
Time to press the button.
My brain is stuck on,
Not listening to tired reason.
Wanting to recharge,
Replenish and refresh.
Yet overloaded with order.
Tasks outstretched.
When will my switches
Be manual to my touch.
To turn on and off
Would be divine.
The time has come
To flick the switches off.
Take control.
Rewire my brain.
Or maybe just take a pill.
Illuminate the cause.
Fade into darkness
And start again.

WHY?

Your touch was like ice.
A shock to my skin,
You were repulsive.
How could you
Steal it from me?
You caused me pain,
Crept into my mind,
Haunted my thoughts,
Stalked my dreams.
I saw you in the shadows,
Under closed eyes.
You are the devil
In an innocent fragile disguise.
You took from me
My childhood naivety.
Replaced it with fear
And anxiety.
Why did you abuse my trust?
Why did you abuse me?
Why did you?
Why?

Victim

She walked into college,
Head held high,
Bible under arm,
Cross visible atop her cardie.
Her bright optimism
Blinded her
To harsh comments,
Her peers disapproving looks.
She handed out leaflets
In the name of God Almighty.
Smiling,
Oblivious,
She continued.
Until he crossed her path.
He wasn't a believer.
He was hurting inside out.
Her cheery god-like nature
Got under his skin.
Glistening sharply
On stolen light,
It only took one second
To thrust the knife into her heart.
Her light left her.
Her body lay still.
Was her religion
A reason to be killed?

A Memory of Me

I would like to fade away
With every drop of rain.
A memory of me left,
Not bitter or sad,
But filled with joy.
I wish I was useful.
If I could take away the pain,
I'd contribute to life.
Not hinder or break.
I wish I was stronger.
My weakness is a drain.
It takes away our smiles.
Replaces mine with shame.
I wish I was another
Who would be bright and never fade.
Yet the memory of me is so pale,
I will fade away.
So when the rain drops drizzle
Upon the window pane,
Don't let your tears comfort them.
Smile through the pain.

Life's Journey

It pushes and crushes,
Rushing along
As you climb a mountain.
It'll shove you back down.
It'll hurt you.
Desert you.
Rip you to shreds.
Make you feel empty.
Scramble your head.
It'll make you feel battered and
Bruised from within.
Break your heart,
And get under your skin.

Life's many battles
Can take their toll.
Yet the longer you survive,
The stronger you are.
So look to the future.
Let optimism be your guide.
And on this life journey
You're sure to thrive.

A Man without a Home

A pile of rotten boxes
Lies on the ground,
Untouched and decayed.
Yet beneath their rotten core,
A lifeless body
Can be found.
A person once passed.
A person who was homeless.
A person with a tormented past.
He walked the streets.
He was alone.
Begged for money.
Longed for a home.
But one day
He got tired.
Tired of this world.
Wanting to sleep forever,
He lay on the ground.
People piled rubbish on him,
Pretending he was not there.
Even when he whimpered,
They still showed no care.
And so his soul left forever.
He escaped from this cruel world,
But his corpse lay still,
Never to be noticed.
These people are ignored,
But they are still there.
Maybe it would be different
If somebody cared.

Answers

She saw the world through other eyes.
The words she spoke
Were often lies.
Her steps she stole
From paths once taken.
Her finger prints were blank.
Identity mistaken.
When she passed by
Your spine would shiver.
For if you look
You will not see her.
She's the pimple on your skin,
The tickle in your tummy.
Deep within
Watch for what you do not see,
Because she will be watching,
Knowing what your future will be.

Behind My Pen

No one wants me
Pushing the writers' pen.
I am too serious.
Bleak and controversial.
I am a taboo.
Unspoken.
I am ignored.
Never questioned.
My voice is silenced,
My words unheard.
They may not see me
But I am still there.
I am war, illness and devastation.
I am death, eating disorders,
Bereavement and starvation.

They crave laughter,
Fun and joy.
Happy endings.
To escape their lives.
Oblivious to the issues
Of another day.

But I remain,
Chipping away.
My point of view
Will be heard.
My chance will come.
To make them think
Of the world beyond
The writers ink.

Prejudice And Pride

www.ingramcontent.com/pod-product-compliance
Lightning Source LLC
Chambersburg PA
CBHW031221290326
41931CB00035B/665